LOVE'S
GOT A LOT TO DO WITH IT!

FOUR
SHORT STORIES

STEVEN LUNDQUIST

Printed in the United States of America

ISBN 979-8-89114-163-6 (sc)
ISBN 979-8-89114-164-3 (e)

Library of Congress Preassigned Control Number: 2025902548

2025.03.19

MainSpring Books
5901 W. Century Blvd
Suite 750
Los Angeles, CA, US, 90045

www.mainspringbooks.com

Synopsis

JOHNNY'S ANGEL

This dark and deeply tragic story finds a crowd gathered at a small town mortuary, waiting for a mobster to arrive to grieve the death of his young wife. The crowd is shocked by the absolute disintegration of the husband's nerve and resolve, until an overwhelming expression of love affects the lives of all who witness this miracle of resurrection.

THE SAGE OF SANTA MONICA

An old man, suffering through an unfathomable feeling of guilt and despair, is comforted by a mysterious little girl who believes that she was sent by God to help save him from himself. As his awareness grows stronger, he realizes that he's been called to make the ultimate sacrifice to save the soul of the little girl.

THE PRESIDENT'S DAUGHTER

On the eve of the most frightening conflict in our nation's history, the President is confronted with a disturbing secret concerning a daughter that he never knew existed. The emotional tension within the conference room explodes through intense confrontations, with surprising consequences that no one in the room could have seen coming.

THE LOVERS

A wild ride that begins shortly after the tragic death of a young husband-to-be on the way to his wedding. His bride-to-be eventually regains her resolve and begins to pick up the pieces of her life in a most dramatic and often lascivious manner. Be aware that portions of this story may be somewhat x-rated.

Johnny's Angel

"He's on his way! Get back, give him some room! Everybody, please! Move away from the door! Give him some room! Come on, people, let's move it! Johnny's on his way! Did you hear me? Johnny's coming! Johnny's coming! Johnny's coming!"

The word spread rapidly. The small, local mortuary was packed to five times its capacity. There was no room to sit, very little room to stand, and absolutely no room to breathe.

Gawky, histrionic maidens enmeshed with haughty, unapproachable dowagers. Bankers brushed against derelicts. Pedants philosophized with petty thieves. Differences could wait until tomorrow. The town was galvanized. One of their own had been taken from them; and not just anybody.

All eyes turned toward the front door. Two or three in the crowd were shaking with grief; yet others were simply curious, insanely curious. A teenaged girl wondered aloud, "How will Johnny act? I mean, will his dignity be like ... you know ... like compromised?" Others wondered, "Will he stumble?" Will he crawl?" Will he whimper?" His friends stated emphatically that Johnny was a man, and that he'd act like a man and keep his emotions to himself.

But, regardless of how they really felt, all agreed that it was in their best interests to be there. Somebody might take notice of their absence. It might be interpreted as a sign of disrespect, or perhaps even guilt. (God forbid!) For Johnny's wife, an angel of barely nineteen, had been cut down by an unknown assassin. A bullet, probably meant for Johnny, had taken the life of the most beautiful girl in town, and somebody was going to have to pay.

The door swung open. Necks craned, eyes bugged out, audible gasps choked the last few drops of breathable air. A shadow of a man, pale, emaciated, walked in. It was Johnny. At least, it kind of looked like Johnny. But Johnny was tall, powerful, and supremely arrogant. This man was frail and sickly. In fact, it looked to the crowd that he was about to keel over.

Johnny knew where he was. He had entered the mortuary. He didn't remember how he got there, but so what? He was there.

He surveyed the crowd. It appeared to him that they were all screaming at him: "Kill him!" "Crucify the bastard!" "The son-of-a-bitch got what's coming to him!" "Hang the motherfucker!" The sound was deafening, overpowering. Johnny's head started racing.

He struggled to maintain his balance. He must have been hallucinating, though, because no one had said a word. Nobody dared. It was stone silence.

Johnny's eyes pierced through the crowd to a small room in the back. The room seemed to beckon him. The Sirens within called out to him in a beautiful Cathedral of sound. He walked quickly toward the room, or so he thought. His concentration was shattered by a smattering of derisive laughter. He looked down to see his legs churning, but he hadn't budged. Not an inch. Then his knees buckled, and he collapsed on the hardwood floor.

What happened next is still subject to interpretation. Some say that he crawled all the way to the accursed room. Others say that he was helped to his feet by a mysterious stranger. The stranger, according to this line of thinking, had just arrived in town when he noticed all the commotion at the mortuary. Apparently, this aroused his curiosity, and he followed Johnny inside. Some say that he helped Johnny to his feet and then disappeared. Others say that he walked with Johnny, supporting him as needed. But all agree that he was never seen again.

Johnny arrived at the viewing room and began to whimper. His hand visibly shook as he reached for the doorknob. The crowd stood transfixed, shocked that Johnny had so completely fallen apart over the murder of his wife. For Johnny was a tough son-of-a-bitch; the meanest, cruelest enforcer this town had ever seen.

Yet even tough guys like Johnny have been known to crumble under the weight of such total devastation, such finality.

A voice from the crowd pleaded with him: "Don't go in there, Johnny. There's nothing to accomplish." Another cried: "She's gone, Johnny. Don't do this to yourself." But Johnny wasn't listening. He couldn't hear them anymore. He gathered his courage and, with his hand still shaking, slowly pushed the door open. There on her bed, asleep so peacefully, his young wife lay forever.

He took a moment to survey the room. A single chair, the casket, some flowers, nothing more. Satisfied that he was alone, he stepped inside and locked the door behind him. But as he turned to gaze at his beloved, a horrible chill overcame him, and he stumbled to the floor in terror. His wife was now standing in front of her casket, smiling at him!

"I've been waiting for you, Johnny."

Johnny recoiled, in horror.

"But … I watched you die!"

"Death is only on the surface, Johnny. Everything else is life."

"You can't really be alive. I'm hallucinating."

"Even that would be enough, Johnny, if it brought us together."

"Don't do this to me, baby. I can't take this kind of cruelty."

"Cruelty is being apart. I couldn't take that either."

"But what am I supposed to do?"

"Johnny, listen to me ... we don't have much time. I want you to come with me. It's the only way for us to be together now."

"Oh God, I want to be with you. But how do I know that we won't be separated again?"

"Because I'm with you now, Johnny. I won't let anything happen to you."

"Then let's go, baby."

Johnny shot up from the floor. He seemed to have regained his strength and resolve.

"Yeah, let's do it, baby. I'm as ready as I'll ever be."

But a stabbing sense of anger now began to surface as he remembered what got him into this position in the first place.

"But, before I go, there's one last thing I need to take care of."

Johnny reached inside his coat and felt for his gun.

"You can't, Johnny. You won't be allowed to come with me."

"He's out there laughing at me! I know who it is now. I can see so clearly now."

"When you come with me, darling, you'll see everything."

"Just tell me if I'm right," he begged. "Was it Petie ... my goddamned best friend?"

With tenderness beyond human understanding, his wife replied, "If you come with me, you'll love Petie as much as you love me. Petie brought us together in a way that no one could have imagined. Without Petie, we wouldn't have been together for long. I never could have accepted your violent life, and your ego would never have allowed you to change. Johnny, don't you see that this was meant to be? It's the only way; but you have to let go."

"I can't let him get away with this."

"Leave it, Johnny. It's God's time for justice, not yours."

But Johnny wasn't listening. All that mattered to him now was his overwhelming desire for revenge. His hand was still shaking as he pulled out his gun.

His wife looked at him with profound tenderness.

"I love you, Johnny. I love you more than I ever loved anything in life."

Her words cut directly to Johnny's soul. He began to cry, softly.

"But you were so young. You never had a chance."

"I fulfilled my destiny, Johnny. I was born to love you."

Johnny's heart went out to his beautiful, young wife.

"Maybe I was born to love you, too," he sobbed.

But suddenly, inevitably, as if her time with Johnny had been only a temporary but precious gift, the bond was broken. Almost imperceptibly, she began to fly away from her husband. Delicately, gracefully, confidently, up through the ceiling, up to the rafters.

"Then follow me, Johnny," she said, as she looked down at him from high above. "Do it now, my darling. It's the only way."

Johnny watched his wife fly away from him, and he knew that he couldn't live without her. He was a thug when he met her, a hopeless loser. Without her, that's all he'd ever be. She brought something noble into his life, something beautiful, and now it was over.

After a few moments, he slumped down on the floor and leaned back against the wall. He was calm now. It all made sense. His destiny was in his hands once again. Slowly, he brought the gun up to his temple and cocked the trigger. For a moment his eyes closed, and he imagined opening the door and smiling at the astonished crowd. He scanned the room for his best friend.

"Hi, Petie. Glad to see you could make it."

"Johnny! Thank God, I was worried about you. You're back to your old self again."

"I'm back, Petie, and I've got a surprise for you."

Johnny pulled out his gun and shot Petie between the eyes. He imagined looking up at his angel, flying high above the crowd. Her tears were falling on his hand. He heard himself saying to her, "I'll be all right. I'm young. I'll find somebody else … in time."

"But I won't, Johnny. I won't find somebody else."

He watched her fly backwards and upward, her right hand stretched out, as if reaching for him for the last time, eternal sadness in her eyes.

A soft knock on the door brought Johnny back to reality.

"Are you all right, Johnny? We're starting to worry about you out here."

"Yeah, I'm all right. Leave me alone."

Johnny looked up at the coffin, where his wife lay so peacefully. He thought of his mom and dad, who tried so hard to get him to go to church. He remembered what he was always taught: that suicides would never be allowed into heaven. He figured the odds at about six to one against him, maybe more. But then again, he thought, maybe love can lower the odds. Maybe even Johnny can get to heaven.

An explosion came from the small room. Everybody knew what it meant. Johnny had buckled. He had taken the coward's way out. Several of the men lunged for the door, but it was locked. Nobody could find the key, so they kicked the door in. The crowd heaved forward to peer at the ghastly sight.

What happened next transcended fear and chaos. During the next few months, grown men who had witnessed the events of that day were known to have broken down in fits of uncontrollable sobbing. For those close to the door swore that Johnny's wife had left her casket and was kneeling over Johnny's lifeless body, tenderly cradling his blood-spattered head in her arms. She was speaking to him in a heavenly language that no one in the room had heard before. Within moments, though, after noticing the crowd, she crawled back into her lifeless body in the casket.

Fortunately, a professor of ancient languages was one of the men who helped break down the door. He later testified that he believed the language spoken by the dead woman was the original language, and perhaps even a modification of the original words, spoken by Adam to Eve.

He couldn't remember, word for word, what had been spoken in the mortuary on that tragic day (after all, there was a lot of commotion); but he stated, with some certainty, that he had been able to translate, with reasonable accuracy, a single phrase that the dead woman had repeated many times over. Here, to the best of his knowledge and ability, is the translation:

"Believe … believe … believe, my love.

"Oh, Johnny … just believe.

"God's love is our love.

"Believe, my husband, just believe.

"He who believes, though he were dead, yet shall he live."

THE END

The Sage Of Santa Monica

"I am," whispered the old man. "I am," came the reply from his reflection in the window.

The old man peered through the window into the night. It was the blackest night he had ever seen. Pure, warm rain appeared to be falling on the other side of his oversized picture window, and yet the wind was lashing at his throat. Was he dry? Was he cold? He wasn't sure, for he could no longer tell to which side of the window he belonged.

He lodged in a small room in the basement of a lonely middle-class home. He had no possessions except for a few clothes; and yet he lacked for nothing, for he had long ago thrown off the entrapments of this world.

His thoughts raced back through a thousand lifetimes: the audacity of his youth, the homogenization of middle-age, the loneliness of old age. He had lived long enough to know that he knew nothing; therefore he knew everything. His abject weakness was his absolute strength. He was worthy in God's eyes. That was enough.

"All my life I've been a singer of songs," he whispered, "a minstrel wandering in the wilderness."

"A minstrel wandering in the wilderness," replied his reflection.

The old man drew closer to the window. "Tell me, if you have the nerve ... where will it end?"

"It will end, singer of songs, in the bowels of hell."

The old man instinctively jerked his body away from the window, for his reflection had suddenly turned grotesque. The mirror of my soul, he thought. God help me.

And as night disappeared into day, the old man disappeared into the night. Doomed, as he believed, to wander in everlasting darkness and solitude, he had descended into the outer edge of insanity: into the eternal fires of remorse, the overwhelming awareness of his sins.

"I am," spouted his reflection. On its head sat the foppish cap of a court jester. An enormous pink mask, dripping with rhinestones, covered its eyes and half of its face. An oversized harmonica appeared to have been jammed into its mouth. A cornucopia of foul music and stale jokes filled the air ... off key, strident, and obscene. "I am, I am, I am," mocked his reflection, now brazenly spitting out torrents of laughter.

The old man's mind became a whirlwind of buffoonery: fragments of long discarded melodies dripping with insipid poetry; sour notes clinging to second-rate songs; and laughter: voluptuous, addictive, and demonic, flowing into his veins. "I am, I am, I am, I am." His reflection pounded his senses into senselessness.

The cacophony of laughter and music, rancid with the stench of hedonistic revelry, overwhelmed the old man. He felt that his brain was about to burst through his skull. No man should ever have to face his reflection, he thought. Nothing could be worse than this.

The old man knelt before God, for only God could save him now. "This is what I am, this is what I am, this is what I am," shouted his reflection.

The old man was ashamed to beg. He would have done almost anything to stop the pain, but begging was unacceptable. "I'm an honest man living an honest life," he declared. "There will be no begging tonight."

In an instant, a crescendo of subterranean thunder burst into the old man's skull, shattering his eardrums like glass. His reflection had torn through the window and grabbed him by the throat. He couldn't breathe; he couldn't think. For the first time he felt the icy fingers of death.

"Behold, your true God!" screamed his reflection. The old man's body contorted into the throes of death, as the fangs of Lucifer, throbbing with venom, shook him by the neck like a dog with a new toy. He was aware only of his impending death. All sensation had left, except for the vague awareness of a persistent tapping in the distance. He would surrender to Lucifer: past, present, and future. What choice did he have?

As he released his soul, the persistent tapping transmuted into the ringing of bells: joyful, exultant, filling his senses, demanding his return to life, elevating his soul into an ever-expanding chorus of glorious sound from which nothing discordant could spring, not even the supreme chaos of Lucifer himself. With the fallen angel in retreat, the old man collapsed into blessed silence. The ringing of bells had subsided into the softest of lullabies: a gentle, persistent tapping on his door.

The old man awoke with a start. Had he dreamed all of this? Outside, the wind was whistling into the warm, black night. He jumped to his feet and glanced at the window. His reflection was benign. The room was awash with silence. Or was it? Within the silence he could hear a faint tapping. So quiet, he thought. So delicate.

As he listened he felt his heart breaking, for the tapping told a tale of unspeakable sadness: the tale of God's lost and oppressed. He walked quickly across the room and put his ear to the door. The soft, sweet singing of birds drifted through the wood. How strange, he thought, for birds to be singing in the middle of the night.

The tapping continued with an occasional short, questioning pause. The tapper was waiting for a response. The old man released the lock and the door swung open. A little girl with long, blond hair looked up at him with amazement. She was dressed in her finest Sunday morning clothes.

"You're very old, aren't you," she said.

"Yes, I am. But what are you doing here, honey? Where's your mother?"

"My mother is with your mother."

"You're out here by yourself? You must be cold. It's the middle of the night."

"It's warm outside. I think it's summer. The sun is shining in your eyes."

"But I can't see it."

"Then let me see it for you. You can use my eyes."

"Is that why you're here, honey? Did someone send you?"

"My father sent me. May I come inside and visit with you?"

"Of course you may, but first shouldn't you tell me why you're here?"

The little girl walked in and sat down on the old man's comfortable chair.

"Don't you want to see the sunlight? The Devil is a bad man. He makes singing bad, but I like singing. Will you sing to me?"

The old man looked around the room. On a small table in the corner sat the two most gentle instruments in the world: a one-inch harmonica and a ukulele. He picked up the ukulele and sat down on the edge of the bed, across from the little girl. Soft, gently strummed harmonies filled the air as the old man began to sing.

"If you were the only girl in the world ..."

The little girl's eyes filled with the timeless wonder of romance and joy, as if she were truly the only girl in the world.

The old man finished his song and, while still strumming, placed the harmonica on the edge of his lips. The pure, soaring tones of "Moonglow" filled the room. Then he looked into the little girl's eyes and began to sing,

"I don't know why ..."

When he had finished singing, the little girl threw back her head and laughed to the sheer joy and magic of the old man's song. "You don't know why you love me like you do."

"But I do know why. I love you because you're the prettiest little girl I've ever known, and I'm very old."

The little girl smiled her happy, innocent smile. She was flattered. But her eyes turned sad as she remembered that summer only comes once, that little girls grow up, that her song had ended. She stood up and, without a word, walked out the door into the night.

The old man knew that it was not his time to follow. He watched from the window as she walked down the driveway and disappeared in the dark. He was not afraid for her, for she was not of this world. But his heart went out to her. Thank Heaven for little girls, he whispered.

He glimpsed another figure through the window: the faint outline of a young woman lingering at the end of the driveway. She seemed reluctant to come closer. He walked over to his open doorway and called out to her. "Are you here to help me see the sunlight?"

Her voice was warm and soothing. "Why shouldn't you see the sunlight? The Devil is no match for God. Just decide to take your mind back. Once you decide, it's done."

As she began to fade into the night, he called out again. "Wait, don't leave yet. I think I know you."

"I didn't want you to see me; it means that you're too close to the other side. It's not your time yet. I shouldn't be here. I have to go."

"Please ... at least tell me about the little girl. Who is she? She broke my heart. I've never known the depth of sadness that she feels in her little heart."

"She was molested and killed in a field behind her church on a beautiful summer's day many years ago. Her parents were inside, worshiping. They didn't miss her until it was too late.

"She's God's favorite. Her first words after she died were, 'Father, forgive him. He didn't know what he was doing.' Even in Heaven, she's never known a moment of happiness since she died."

"My God, will she be all right?"

"You're right to ask God. I don't know what to tell you. More tears have been shed in Heaven for her than for anyone else. She believes that she was sent here to save you; but, really, she was sent here so that you could save her. That's the way God works. When you sang your loving, gentle songs you entered her mind and made her feel alive and good and free. That's your gift. That was always your gift."

"Why were you watching me? Don't leave without telling me the truth. In Heaven's name, who are you?"

"I've said too much. We're not allowed to interfere; there are strict rules about this."

"Then how will I ever escape this darkness? Is my life simply a monument to vanity and ego?"

"I won't be your judge. All of creation seeks its creator. Seek God with your last drop of blood. That's the only reason for living. With every breath, with every tear, with every smile, with every song, seek God ... until God seeks you."

And she was gone. The old man stepped back inside his little apartment and closed the door behind him. His personal hell had continued for several days. He was determined now to regain control of his mind.

The battlefield was clearly marked. The Devil promotes chaos, he thought, but God is clarity. God is the child within each of us, the purity of spirit that sees only sunlight. To this child I once dedicated my life. I must not fail him now.

The old man waited for the sunlight. He sat down on his comfortable chair and waited and waited until, finally, he collapsed in sheer emotional exhaustion. He began to dream. He dreamed that he had been anointed king; of what, he wasn't quite sure. Perhaps of a mythical country; perhaps only of his neighborhood.

His subjects were the birds and flowers outside his window. He was a benign king, loved by children everywhere. Music and laughter overflowed the boundaries of his kingdom. Sunlight from perpetually blue skies radiated within.

A faint rattling of leaves disturbed the old man's dream. He awoke with a sense of foreboding. Something terrible was hovering outside his door. He waited in silence for the knock until three resounding thuds demolished his door into kindling.

He stood up and walked over to the now unprotected entrance. A tall, dignified man, ageless and impenetrable, stood on the threshold. He was dressed in a black suit and black tie. His pointed, black shoes were huge. He spoke in deep, rich tones.

"So you'd like to see the sunlight," he said. "Allow me to introduce myself. I was once God's right hand, but I had the extreme pleasure of being hurled out of his kingdom. I traveled at the speed of light. In my eyes I carried the magnificence of the sun. I'm the Sorcerer, the one most feared."

"Lucifer," whispered the old man, instinctively drawing back. "I have no defense. Take me if you must."

"I have no intention of taking you. I thought we might have a little chat."

"What could I possibly have to offer you?"

"Nothing whatsoever. I feast on rabble like you. I ravage the souls of the weak, the bile of the earth, and it turns my stomach. To feast on human detritus is my eternal humiliation. I'm not interested in you personally, but you're going to help me get what I want."

"I refuse to help you. I would appreciate if you would leave my home."

"You have the gift of intuition. A few of the rabble have had it, but proportionally an infinitesimal amount. I can give you names: Einstein, DaVinci, Bach. But others have been much like you: nameless, faceless ... living desultory lives, unfocused, uneventful ..."

"You discount the significance of my family and, equally, my extended family."

"Yes, I do. Family is simply a manifestation of morality, a formula for effecting the known virtues. You allow yourself to believe that it's all about love. How endearingly silly.

"You're an emotional maggot. You have no capacity for love and you know it. Family is a primer, a remedial course in loveless propriety and discipline.

"I know love. Love is the primordial source, but hate is so much better. You should really try some good old-fashioned hate sometime instead of this burdensome self-loathing. Hate is love with an attitude."

"What do you want from me?"

"I want the little girl."

"You can't have her. I'll defend her with my life."

"She lives in Paradise, and yet she's desperately unhappy. Doesn't it strike you as odd?"

"Why do you ask? Does it strike you as odd?"

"Of course not. You make me laugh. You know my history too well. What you fail to perceive is that God will not permit this aberration in his kingdom. We should all be clones with happy faces. The little girl will not survive under these conditions. I'll have her anyway. You can expedite her delivery."

"Do you really believe that I could ever betray a child?"

"The child is lost. You cannot save her."

"I disagree."

"Haven't you taken enough punishment? I know your weaknesses so well. If you refuse to do as I ask, I'll cast you into the pit of vipers. They'll feed on your brain. You won't even remember the little girl."

"There's a force much greater than the pit of vipers: the force of indignation. You will not have the little girl. Her soul will become my soul. I'll protect her throughout eternity."

"Then I'll let you rot in your own delusions. Sing merrily, singer of songs, while I rip your tongue from your mouth. Suck your harmonica while I drain the blood from your lips. Learn to live with subtraction. I'll take your mind and your body, piece by piece."

"Why do you insist on taking this innocent child?"

"She's not as innocent as you think. She humiliated me at the moment of her death. Her remark was unfair and unprecedented. I wasn't even interested in her. I was pursuing her defiler: a family man, a pillar of his community; her Sunday school teacher, no less.

"In spite of her pitiful request, he came straight to me at his death. I elected to fry him face down in scalding oil. The poor man severely singed his eyeballs. If you listen closely you can hear him screaming."

The old man shook his head in disgust. "If I listen much longer I'll be screaming along with him. This discussion is over. I must ask you to leave."

He gathered his courage and walked over to the window where he glanced, painfully, at his reflection. But the foolish, toothless clown from his dream was nowhere to be seen. The window now reflected determination and strength.

He leaned up close and looked deep into his own eyes. "I have only one request: Don't let him break me without a battle. His logic is stronger than mine. His power of persuasion is terrible to behold. I'll never defeat him by intellect alone. He'll burrow into my wounds and twist the truth to his ends. There must be another way. Help me."

"You were wise to come to me," replied his reflection. "It's the middle of the afternoon and you have yet to see the sunlight. Surely, you wouldn't want your whole day to be covered in darkness."

The old man began to feel the fires of hell ascending through the pit of his stomach. A fierce sphere of bright orange projected through the window. His eyes retracted as if pressed upon by hot pokers. The pain from the glare increased with blazing intensity. "Ahhhhhhh!" he screamed with blood-chilling ferocity.

"I love to work on the eyes," laughed the stranger. "The eyes are so very sensitive. May I assume that you agree? Sunlight is my specialty. The delivery of light and warmth to all mankind is my noble ambition; but, in your case, why wait until the afterlife? Let's proclaim the glory of your emasculation while you're still wriggling. Your state of separation with God is so severe that you have no recourse anyway."

"Why are you hurting him?" shouted the little girl from the end of the driveway. She was on her knees, with her hands clasped together as if in prayer. "He was going to sing for me."

"Of course he'll sing for you. What would you like to hear? I'll make him vomit in the key of C. If I squeeze him hard enough he might even squeal in Pig Latin."

"He won't do bad things. He makes singing good. He sings about love and gentleness, and my house and the trees and my swing. He sings about the sky and warm summer mornings. He sings about my puppy and my treehouse. You're a very bad man. Why don't you leave?"

"I'd be delighted to leave. Perhaps you'd like to come with me."

"My father would never let me come with you."

"Your father doesn't want you. You're not like the others. You belong with me."

A tear rolled down the little girl's cheek. Through the window she could see the old man staring into an imaginary abyss, as if he could no longer see the world around him. A thunderous explosion and the spraying of shattered glass had revealed the awful power of the sun's laserlike rays. Hell had arrived on earth.

From a distance, the old man could feel the little girl's tiny hand in his. "You're a sage, aren't you?" she whispered from her world to his. "That's what wise men are called in Heaven. My father told me that you're a pure sage. He said that you're not pretending like the others. He wanted me to help you. Have I helped you?"

"God, yes." The old man felt the tears start to flow as he realized the power of this child, but he quickly pulled himself together. "Now let me help you."

"Do I need help?"

"Yes, darling, you do."

"He can't help you now," barked the stranger. He was standing outside the shattered window with his arms crossed, obviously pleased with himself. "Direct sunlight has a way of searing the optic nerve. He'll be lucky if he can find his way to the bathroom."

The old man felt the warmth of the little girl's hand. "You have to go back," he said, "and you have to do it now. I don't mean to where you just came from. I mean to where you once lived … to your hometown."

"It's a longshot," said the stranger.

"I only play longshots."

"It'll play out exactly the same. You can't alter the past by simply reliving it."

The little girl seemed puzzled. "How will I find my hometown?"

"I'm going with you," said the old man. "I know exactly where it is."

"But my father might not want me to go."

"Your father wants you to live. That's why he sent you to me."

"You two make a ludicrous pair," interjected the stranger. "I admit that you have an extraordinary idea, but you have no means to follow it through. You'll need a blueprint. You'll need to study various routes and, of course, you'll discover that it's all nonsense anyway. But you've aroused my curiosity. How in the world do you intend to travel back in time? In a spacecraft?"

The old man looked deep into the black hole of his existence and knew that the answer had arrived with the question. "The young woman at the edge of the driveway … just a few minutes ago, after I sang to you. Who is she?"

"I don't think I'm supposed to tell you."

"She's a whore … a mindless twit," murmured the stranger.

"I believe she's an angel," replied the old man, "the only angel I've ever known. She reminded me that life is not merely the struggle, it's the direction of our glance. The child holds the sunlight in his hands. He doesn't attain it; he simply accepts it. The key is to look backward … backward …"

The little girl was now up on her toes at the edge of the driveway, stretching her neck, trying to see the old man. "What should we do?" she pleaded.

"Come over to me and take my hand."

"The bad man is blocking my way,"

"He can't hurt you if you believe in me. Do you believe in me?"

"I believe in you with all my heart."

"Then come to me quickly and put your arms around my neck."

The little girl scampered up the driveway and lunged through the opening created by the sun's rays. The old man caught her and lifted her into his arms.

"Are you blind?" she asked.

"It doesn't matter, sweetheart. I can see much better than before."

"I know where you're going with this," said the stranger. "Humans are God's excrement. They're incapable of original thought unless they tap into the mind of an angel; but you seem to have forgotten that I was God's most powerful angel. It's impossible to outsmart me. You already have one foot in hell; it's just a matter of time until I get the other one."

"You've proven your ignorance with that statement. You survive by distorting the truth. You have no sense of originality. You're nothing but a sorcerer; you said so yourself. You confuse and befuddle and annoy. I'm ashamed to say that I almost allowed you to break me over the past few days; but it ends here."

"I suppose you're right. You're an old man. I'll take her now, over your dead body."

The old man started to stumble. The little girl held on tight, with her arms around his neck. "Do you want me to let go?" she asked.

"Not yet. I want you to remember ... back to that beautiful Sunday morning as you were getting ready for church. I know your hometown very well. I happen to live there now."

"I lived in Santa Monica."

"I know, honey. You never left Santa Monica. In fact, after you died you came right back to your house ... this house. You didn't know where else to go."

"But I thought I was in Heaven, My father talks to me all the time."

"Your father misses you terribly. He wants you to be with him. He waited for you, but somehow you got lost. You and I must have been about the same age when you died. For some reason your spirit entered my body and eventually led me to this house."

"Intuition is a wonderful thing," said the stranger. "You make it up as you go along. Now give her to me and I'll let you live for a few more hours."

"Tell me, sweetheart, where did you go when you left me? Why did you come from the end of the driveway just now?"

"I went to look for my father."

"Will you take me with you next time? I want to talk to him."

"But it's not your time yet."

"I think it is my time. I think that's what this is all about."

"You're a fool," said the stranger. "All humans fear death. It's the most powerful bargaining tool in my arsenal. Why don't you come to your senses and think about extending your life? I might even decide to restore your sight."

"I'm going to set you down now, honey ... I don't have much strength left. From here on out you'll have to be my strength. When I put you down I want you to hold onto my hand and, with your other hand, reach over and pick up the ukulele from the table."

"Do you mean the little guitar?"

"That's right."

"What about the little tiny harmonica?"

"I've already got it. I always try to keep it with me. It's the voice of reason, the song of the child in a world of chaos."

"Where are we going from here?"

"We're going back in time; back to an age of romance, to a time of innocence. All I want you to do now is remember. Think back to your parents and your friends and the laughter in your home. Think of the joy of waking up in your own bed. Think of the beautiful summer days when you ran around in your backyard, playing with your puppy. Think about everything you loved in life.

"Then think of the young prince who will someday come for his princess. Remember the stirrings of romance that had already begun to form in your mind. Listen to me, darling, and remember; for I'm the singer of songs, the keeper of dreams. We'll travel together on my songs."

"If you travel back to her lifetime she'll have to let go of your hand," said the stranger. "Your intuition failed you this time. She died before you were born. You won't be allowed to go with her."

"Did you die before I was born, sweetheart?"

"I think so."

"Of course she did, you idiot. Don't you have any idea who she is?"

"What are you trying to …?"

"The daughter they never talked about."

"My sister?"

"You have to look at this logically. As you release her hand, I'll be there to scoop her up. You can't save her. Just hand her over to me and I'll prolong your miserable life."

The old man gently squeezed the little girl's hand. "Let's you and I agree that we'll never again live in fear. I'll start you on your journey, then you can take it the rest of the way on your own. I know you can do it, sweetheart. Just believe in me; believe in my magic."

The little girl wrapped her arms around the old man's leg as he began to sing while strumming his ukulele. "This could be my time," she thought, "if only I could live."

The little girl's eyes turned to the past as the old man began strumming his beautiful symphony of songs. She remembered back to her last day on earth. She could almost sense the warmth of her bed, the fragrance of her mother's perfume as they dressed for church.

"I want to go back, even if it's just for a little while. Please let me see my world again."

She remembered walking to church on the morning of her death. She lived just down the street, in the parsonage. Her father was the pastor. She loved her church. Everybody was always so friendly and happy.

"It doesn't have to be perfect. Even if I have to die on the very first day, just let me live for as long as I may."

The little girl vanished suddenly. The old man continued strumming his little guitar. He kept strumming and strumming, slower and slower, until he found the strength to coax one last song out of his own broken heart.

"Goodnight sweetheart ... good ..."

The little guitar dropped to the floor with a thud. After a moment, the stranger stepped inside the tiny apartment and gently nudged the lifeless body on the floor. Then he turned and slowly walked out into the warm, summer air.

He had always loved his long, pointed black shoes. He stopped for a moment to admire them. "Win a few, lose a few," he muttered. After allowing himself a brief skyward glance, he tunneled, feet first, directly downward.

THE END

The President's Daughter

Here we go, the old step and slide routine. One … two; One … two; It's hard to hide a bum leg when everybody stops talking and turns to watch you drag the damn thing down the length of the conference room. Damn these bastards! All they care about anyway is saving their own damn ass. There isn't a one of them who has the courage to speak from the heart. They have to do the "right" thing.

Damn the "right" thing! Show us some balls, for Christ's sake! That's what the boss needs to see now. The truth. The truth! Reach inside of yourselves, gentlemen! Find your humanity, for Christ's sake! This is no time for politics!

Ah, to hell with them. They always sound to me like a choir of eunuchs, with their high-pitched whining and belly-aching. I don't know how the boss puts up with these assholes.

Tom Johnson, aide to the President, had finally dragged his bum leg up to the head of the table, and was now whispering something in the President's ear. Strangely, it appeared to be of an inappropriate, personal nature. The President, a model of equanimity, had obviously been caught off guard. He began to breathe in quick little gasps, and one of his eyelids had begun to twitch.

The assembly was perturbed. What could be so damned important that this idiot cripple had to break in on one of the most important meetings in our nation's history? War was imminent. The nation was about to be ripped apart. Was it too late for diplomacy? Of course it was. It was too late for diplomacy six months ago! But the council, composed of eight congressmen and three cabinet members, had now been assembled to debate that very question.

The President's closest advisors insisted that every avenue of diplomacy had been explored. It was time to fight. Others pleaded that diplomacy must never be abandoned. We must continue to reason with our enemies. Yes, they're wrong; but we must convert them, not destroy them.

In spite of what the President's aide believed, both sides were appropriately and passionately committed to their opinions. So much was at stake. The President had turned ashen. He knew that a decision had to be made quickly, and he knew what that decision must be: to preserve the nation at all costs. Yes, war was imminent, but to declare war would mean unbelievable carnage.

And war with whom? Your neighbor, your brother, your son, your …

"Mr. President, the young lady is waiting. May I give her your answer?"

The President, somewhat impatiently, motioned his aide to come closer.

"Mr. Johnson, how long have you known me?"

"A little over four years, Mr. President."

"Tom, you've known me for over four years. What in God's name gave you the wild idea that I have a daughter?"

"Mr. President, with all due respect, you have a daughter and she needs to see you; urgently and immediately, Mr. President."

The President leaned back in his chair, clasped his hands together, and put his knuckles up to his lips. The members of the council could sense that the President was no longer aware of their presence. He was staring intently into the recesses of his own mind.

"Mr. President?"

"Send her in, Mr. Johnson."

"But Mr. President, shouldn't you clear the room first?"

"Mr. Johnson, did you ask me to see her or not? This meeting will not be dispersed. Within the hour, a decision will be made to kill or maim thousands of our finest young men. Families will turn on each other. Homes will be destroyed. Property held for generations will be burned beyond recognition.

"I had a dream, Mr. Johnson. Our young women will be raped. Children will be butchered … all in the name of solidarity. The nation will be preserved at all costs, Mr. Johnson. Now send her in."

"But Mr. President …"

"Send her in, Mr. Johnson."

The President had come up the hard way. From the beginning of their relationship, Mr. Johnson had recognized that the President's gentle facade belied an almost brutal inner toughness. This was not a man to be taken lightly. He had lost too many battles to have continued to be a plausible candidate, but he had persevered.

He certainly wasn't polished as an orator. There was no trace of aristocracy in the man. But this populist thing; how can you figure it? A leader who isn't a leader; just a man. One of the people. But, God, how the people seemed to love him.

Yet very few of the council members truly respected him. They admired his incredible staying power, but they felt that he lacked the passion to be an effective leader. He was a good man, but he lacked the fire. There was no bluster; he was too gentle. He was more of a pacifier.

And, let's face it, he was odd; and homely to boot. And what the hell was he up to now? Now when we're about to make the most important decision of our careers, he interjects some bizarre little drama that appears to be of a personal nature.

The President's aide started his painfully slow journey back to the entrance. One ... two; One ... two; The gentlemen of the council, in perplexed anticipation, had turned in their chairs to watch the aide shuffle back to the door when all hell broke loose. Mrs. Lincoln, the President's wife, flew into the room from the courtyard outside, screeching and bellowing like an alley cat.

"Where is she, you son-of-a-bitch? I know she's here! Don't you think I know what's going on around here? I'm going to claw her beady little eyes out of their sockets!"

"Perhaps we should address this at another time, my dear," said the President.

"I want her now! Now!" cried Mrs. Lincoln, at the top of her voice. "I'm going to kill her, you weasel! You slimy weasel! You're a traitor! A traitor!" she screamed, before breaking down into sobs. The President's aide tried to console her by putting his arms around her, but Mrs. Lincoln broke free and jumped up onto the long conference table where she ran unimpeded from side to side, hissing and spitting at the council members.

The gentlemen of the council had, of course, all jumped to their feet at her arrival and were now staring at her in horror. The biggest and burliest of the group, a Senator McClelland, the President's primary adversary on practically every issue, had a particularly annoying problem. It seems that, in the extreme shock of the moment, he had wet his pants. This was most embarrassing because, unfortunately, at the split second that he had noticed his predicament, two or three of his fellow council members had noticed as well.

The President, though, had regained his composure. The color had returned to his cheeks. He was now prepared for war, albeit only with his wife.

"My dear, we'll discuss this later. I have a most important meeting to attend to. It cannot be delayed any further. I'm asking you to come down from the table and I'll escort you to your carriage."

Mrs. Lincoln was tired. What a terrible strain for a Thursday afternoon. She longed to return to her knitting. She had been working on a quilt for her sickly son, Tad. Such a dear boy. I wonder if he's getting hungry. It's late. I want to go home.

The President extended his hand. Mrs. Lincoln grabbed hold and, with exaggerated unsteadiness, stepped down first to the chair vacated by Senator McClelland and, finally, to the ground. With a nod from the President, Mr. Johnson stepped in to escort Mrs. Lincoln to her carriage. This time, however, the suddenly docile Mrs. Lincoln allowed herself to be consoled by the somewhat embarrassed young man.

The President and each of the council members watched in silence as Mrs. Lincoln and the President's aide made their unsteady journey back to the entrance. One ... two; One ... two; But as the aide opened the door, Mrs. Lincoln calmly turned back to her audience for a parting shot.

"I know what you do in this room. You're Devil worshipers, all of you. Satan has his hand in these meetings. Now you're going to destroy our country … our beautiful, beautiful country. You should pray to God, gentlemen. Pray to God to save yourselves; to save our country; to save me!"

Mrs. Lincoln broke down and started to sniffle. The President gestured for the aide to quickly remove her from the room and escort her to her carriage.

"The Devil is a she, gentlemen," yelled Mrs. Lincoln from the courtyard. "Protect yourselves! She's right here on earth, on these very grounds!"

"Mr. Johnson!" the President called out.

"Yes, Mr. President?"

The President couldn't bear to utter the words that his wife longed to hear. This was not the time for personal demonstrations. A clear head and a rational mind was imperative. The fate of our nation was at stake.

"Mr. President?"

"Be kind to her, Mr. Johnson."

"Of course, Mr. President."

The President walked over to the doorway and closed the door. The council members, frozen in place, stared at the President, at the door, at the apparition of Mrs. Lincoln. What just happened here? How could this be? Why should we have been subjected to the ramblings of a deranged woman?

The President turned to face his tribunal. "Gentlemen, we have more important things to attend to. I beg you, take your seats."

The council members took their places at the table as the President quickly walked back to the head of the table and took his seat.

"Gentlemen," began the President, "we all know that slavery is the real issue here. I believe, and I would hope that you also believe, that all men are created equal. I believe that personal freedom is the right of every man, woman, and child. I believe that each man has the right to choose his own destiny. I believe that importing free men from Africa and forcing them to be our slaves is an abomination in God's eyes."

"How do you feel about women, Mr. President?"

The voice came from the doorway. It belonged to a young woman of perhaps thirty; a woman of intense physical beauty, with iridescent eyes, dark complexion, and burning sexual intensity. Two or three of the more vocal members jumped to their feet and demanded an explanation for these personal interruptions.

"Senator McClelland," said the young woman, noticing the stain on the white haired gentleman's trousers, "would you like to go home and change, or are you quite comfortable?"

"I'm quite comfortable."

"Then sit down, Senator McClelland. All of you, sit down."

The bewildered council members once again took their seats.

"You haven't answered my question, Mr. President," the young woman persisted.

President Lincoln slumped back in his chair, folded his hands on his abdomen, and stared at the table in front of him, waiting for the other shoe to drop.

"Mr. President, how do you feel about women?"

"I adore them."

"Of course you do, Mr. President, as well you should. You're a red-blooded American male. It was to be expected that, in your youth, you would begin a dalliance with a negro woman; a slave woman by the name of Jesse. An acquaintance of yours, whom you had met strictly by chance, treated you to the pleasures of one of his many slaves.

"It was common practice in those days. It's nothing to feel ashamed about, Mr. President. For three years you treated this lovely woman with warmth and even, in your own naive way, respect. Your sense of decency caused Jesse to fall in love with you; and, I believe, from the stories I've heard, that you may have loved her too.

"But one day you disappeared. Not a word was said; not goodbye, not I'll miss you, not have a good life, not thank you for loving me. Jesse was ordered back to her master's bed, but this time he toyed with her. Her heart was broken and he tortured her by telling her that you had never loved her, that it was just a game. He didn't like you, Mr. President, and the word was out that you couldn't stand him either. It was understood that you only tolerated him because of your love for Jesse.

"Jesse was humiliated, beaten, and tortured for several weeks until her pregnancy began to show and the master moved on to another, younger slave girl. In time, he moved on to me. It surprises you, gentlemen! Why would the master choose a white girl when a legion of beautiful slave girls were there for his bidding? Well, look again, gentlemen. I was thirteen when the master ordered me to his bed. I came prepared with a small knife with a very sharp blade. The master died in his sleep that night.

"Gentlemen, let me introduce myself. My name isn't important. I've had many names; I've had many lovers. All that need concern you now is that I, too, like Jesse, am the daughter of a slave. The look of incredulity in your eyes is somewhat amusing to me, gentlemen. Why would a white woman in her right mind attempt to pass herself off as black? The answer, gentlemen, is that I am black. My light skin is simply a prop to be used to enhance my skill as an actress.

"I think you understand by now that I'm not your typical negro illiterate. I'm an attorney as well as a professional actress. I'm reasonably wealthy and I certainly don't need your charity. My current name, if you must know, is Karen Booth. I'm married to an actor from a well-known family of actors. He's unaware of my past, my race, and my involvement with the President."

Senator McClelland jumped to his feet. "Mr. President, must we continue with these sordid confessions while the fate of our nation rests in our hands?" Oh dear, he thought, as he felt the warmth flowing into his trousers once again. How will anyone ever take me seriously again?

"Please sit down, Senator McClelland," demanded the determined young woman. "Have patience, gentlemen. I promise you that within five minutes you'll come to realize, as I have, that the fate of the nation rests not in your hands but in mine.

"I mentioned my involvement with the President. Several weeks ago I ingratiated myself to the President. I met him at a fund-raising dinner at the White House. Perhaps some of you gentlemen will now remember me from the party that followed. I openly flirted with the President. You may recall that his wife was furious, but the President found it impossible to resist my advances.

"You see, gentlemen, I was not to be denied. My affair with the President had been carefully planned for weeks, and not just by me. Many of my friends and colleagues were involved, for we would have been paralyzed without the information that only the President could possibly have known, namely what was he going to do and when? The only one who was not involved, for obvious reasons, was my husband. Because of his extremely violent and jealous nature he must never know.

"And so, gentlemen, the President and I began a torrid love affair; and with the physical release, the emotional release was soon to follow. He learned to trust me with his most secret and sensitive thoughts. That's why I'm here today, gentlemen. The President must be stopped!

"He's duplicitous. He preaches to you that the nation must be preserved at all costs, and yet three nights ago he conspired with the enemy to maintain the status quo until arrangements can be made to split the United States into two separate countries. This meeting is a sham! He has agreed to stall the proceedings to initiate the war until the South can build its army and arsenal up to parity with the North!"

The members of the council all jumped to their feet and began shouting. Not a one could have remembered even minutes later what he had said, what he had thought. For a few terrible seconds, chaos reigned. The President remained silent as he continued to stare at the table in front of him. The young Mrs. Booth regained control through the sheer force of her determination.

"Gentlemen, look at me. Look at me! Come to your senses, gentlemen. Your country demands your rapt attention!"

Some of the men collapsed in their chairs. Others remained standing as if waiting for directions. All were depleted and confused.

"Sit down, gentlemen," ordered Mrs. Booth. "I have the only solution at hand."

The members of the council stared in horror, for Mrs. Booth was pointing her pistol at the President. One of the older members of the council, a Senator Stevens, a man known to have a kind heart and a calm nature, intervened.

"Young lady, this is madness. Put down your pistol and leave us to deal with this. You've done your part well. There's nothing more that you can do."

"I cannot leave, gentlemen, until this man is deposed or dies in front of me," replied Mrs. Booth. "I've devoted my life to the pursuit of my own personal freedom. Now I'm prepared to give my life, if I must, to the cause of freedom for my race."

"For God's sake, young lady! Don't mercilessly take the life of a man with a noble heart."

"A noble heart, Senator Stevens? What kind of a man would sleep with his own daughter?"

"He certainly wouldn't have known that you were his daughter unless you had told him."

"He knew," insisted Mrs. Booth. "I tell you, he knew. I could see it in his eyes. I could tell by the way he held me in his arms. He knew that I was a part of someone he loved so long ago. He knew that I was the daughter of his Jesse; the love child of the future President and a lowly, despicable slave woman."

Mrs. Booth never wavered throughout this dialogue. Her gun was pointed rigidly, at arm's length, at the head of the President. She was in a position to see the whole room in front of her: the President sitting facing her, with his hands folded and his head bowed, staring thoughtfully at the table in front of him; the gentlemen of the council turned sideways in their chairs, staring at her intently; the President's aide, Mr. Johnson ... Mr. Johnson! She had almost forgotten about him.

Mr. Johnson had introduced her to the President. At the time he wasn't aware of her identity, but he had been sympathetic with her desire to meet the President; and this afternoon he had believed her when she told him that she was the President's daughter, though she certainly hadn't confided the whole story. He had even opened the door for her a few minutes ago, allowing her to penetrate the room without being seen. Where is Mr. Johnson, anyway? A cold chill crept up her spine. Something was wrong.

"You're prepared to die, are you?"

It was Mr. Johnson's voice. Mrs. Booth knew immediately that if she wavered even slightly, she would die; or, at the very least, be captured and rendered impotent. She fixed her gaze on the President's forehead, imagining the bullet from her outstretched arm traveling through space into the President's skull. The thought of his skull collapsing made her smile.

From behind her she heard the shuffling. One ... two; One ... two; She felt Mr. Johnson's warm body pressed tightly into her buttocks and thighs, while the cold steel of his revolver indented her temple.

"I've listened to your speech, Mrs. Booth," said Mr. Johnson. "It was most impressive, very dramatic.

But you left something out, didn't you? Something important."

"I don't know what you're talking about," replied Mrs. Booth, now unable to move because of a brutally tight headlock applied by Mr. Johnson.

"You left out that you're a sneaking little shit of a whore who never set foot on a plantation."

President Lincoln stood up from the table. "Let her go, Mr. Johnson."

"You're crazy, you ignorant clubfoot," gurgled Mrs. Booth. "You're choking me! Let go of me ... I'll kill him where he stands!"

"Mr. Johnson, please!" the President cried.

Mr. Johnson's chokehold became more intense. The young woman gasped for air. Her face turned blue. She attempted to pull the trigger, but her strength was waning rapidly. Then suddenly, with a loud and gleeful shout, Mr. Johnson snapped her neck like a twig. The young woman's limp body fell to the floor.

Silence, interspersed with multiple sighs of relief, prevailed over the chamber for the next several minutes. The President collapsed in his chair. The gentlemen of the council slumped down in their chairs. A few of them relaxed the tension by leaning their foreheads against the table in front of them.

Mr. Johnson broke the silence. "It was good that no shot was fired. To my knowledge, nobody saw her enter the grounds. I'm sorry to say that I was the one who unwittingly helped her, Mr. President. I'll take full responsibility for assuring that no one will see the body until it's removed from the premises.

"Gentlemen, I'm going to leave the room for a moment to find something to cover the body. But first, I want the word of every man in this room that no one outside of this chamber will ever know what happened here today. Swear it gentlemen!"

Senator McClelland spoke up. "He's right. No one must ever know the secrets disclosed in this room today; and no one must ever hear of the attempted assassination. The country, in its weakened condition, simply couldn't take it.

"Mr. President, we've had our differences. You know that I've never supported you, and I'm very sorry for that. But I believe that you're a good man. Tell me now, and tell me the God's truth. Have you conspired with a renegade faction to create two separate countries within our borders?"

"Yes, Senator McClelland, I have."

"But your speeches, your actions, all indicate otherwise. Was this sham strictly for political gain?"

The President's answer was interrupted by Mr. Johnson, who had returned to the conference room with a large blanket in his hands. The assembly stared at him and he stared back.

"Go ahead, Mr. President," he said. "I'd like to hear your answer."

"Gentlemen," replied the President, "you all think that you know me, but you don't understand that I'm ill-equipped to make a decision like this. I'm simply incapable of playing God. To decree that our countrymen must slaughter each other in the name of freedom is beyond all limits of humanity."

"Then we'll make the decision for you," said Senator McClelland. "I have never agreed with your rhetoric in the past, Mr. President, but the mood of the country indicates a plurality in favor of declaring war against the South. Gentlemen, I need your vote. The country demands unity! All who agree to maintain the integrity of the United States by any means necessary, including the initiation of an aggressive war against the South, raise your hand. All opposed?" It was unanimous. Plans for war would be implemented immediately.

"And one final thing, gentlemen," declared Senator McClelland. "We must all agree to honor the pact proposed by the President's aide. Gentlemen, each of you must answer. Do you swear on your sacred honor to never tell a living soul what occurred in these chambers this afternoon? If so, raise your right hand and say "I do so swear." The assembly, in unison, repeated "I do so swear."

Mr. Johnson left with the body of Mrs. Booth, which he had wrapped in the blanket. The members of the council, deep in contemplation, filtered out behind him in silence, though two or three of the congressmen could be heard mumbling to each other.

"Of course we'll never tell anyone. This could ruin our careers. Our constituents would never stand for it."

The President found himself alone and devastated. In agony, he dropped to his knees.

"Jesse," he whispered. "Jesse, forgive me. I didn't know. I didn't want to know. I had hoped that Karen was the reincarnation of you, my love. I believed that you had come back to me. I'm so sorry, Jesse, for everything I've done."

The President leaned forward and began to cry, softly.

"Please forgive me. Forgive me."

He cried steadily for ten minutes until he heard the door open.

"Is that you, Tom?" said the President in a hoarse, painful voice.

"On your knees, Mr. President? How unseemly." The voice belonged to Karen.

The President looked up. Mr. Johnson was standing next to Mrs. Booth, who seemed very much alive. Both of them were smiling and in obvious good spirits.

"What an incredible performance, my dear," laughed Mr. Johnson. "You can grace my stage anytime."

"And you can grease my palm anytime, Mr. Johnson," said Mrs. Booth. "It was a nice touch, wasn't it, to use the name Booth. It added a subtle credibility. If I were only so fortunate to really be married to a Booth, my career would be booming by now."

She let out a hearty laugh. "I wonder how long it will take before the famous John Wilkes Booth discovers that his 'wife' had an affair with the President."

"It will probably be a few years before these scared little rabbits start to confess," chuckled Mr. Johnson.

"Mr. President," laughed Mrs. Booth, "this was truly the ultimate test for an actress, to have convinced the whole council that white is really black."

"And to get old McClelland to not only agree with our point of view but to actually lead the charge was well nigh a miracle. You're a wonderful actress, my dear," said Mr. Johnson.

The President, still on his knees, stared in disbelief.

"How can you talk to me like this? What could you possibly have had to gain by dissimulation?"

Mr. Johnson suddenly frowned. "This nation will fall if it perceives that the man in charge is weak. And you, Mr. President, would be vilified. I couldn't let that happen.

"When I saw that you were wavering I hired an actress to get more information. When she brought me the most critical information, that you were obsessed with a dream of annihilation, I knew that you were leaning toward collusion with the renegades of the South to sabotage the inevitable process of war; and I knew that with the support of those weaklings in the council, you could darn well pull it off."

Mr. Johnson paused to let it sink in. "I had to stage a fantastic but plausible story that no one, not even you, Mr. President, could deny with certainty. To do that I went back into the public records. I studied your history. I learned where you lived. I talked to people who knew you in the old days; and, lo and behold, a story came to light about an evil plantation owner who allowed a mere acquaintance to rendezvous with his prized mistress.

"After that, there was a gap in your history. People speculate, but no one knows for sure what happened during the next two years. My theory is that you buckled down with your books and vowed to do everything you possibly could to abolish the blight of slavery from our land. You became a good lawyer, Mr. President, and history will judge you a damn good President."

"There's just one thing I can't understand, Mr. President," said the young lady previously known as Mrs. Booth. "If you truly loved Jesse, why didn't you try to find out what happened to her?"

She paused to wait for the President's answer. None was forthcoming.

"She died, Mr. President, two years after you left her; some say of a broken heart."

The President finally rose from his knees and slowly eased into a chair. He bowed his head and clasped his hands together as if in prayer.

"Mrs. Booth, or whatever your name is, I know all about Jesse. I was there when she died."

Mrs. Booth and the President's aide were taken aback at this disclosure. This had not been uncovered during Mr. Johnson's fact-finding mission.

"She died during childbirth."

"What happened to the baby?" asked Mrs. Booth.

"I bought his freedom, for a handsome price, and placed him in the home of a wonderful family who raised him as their own.

"But enough of this. Tell me, Mr. Johnson, why did you go to all this trouble to sabotage my efforts to save hundreds of thousands of lives? My fellow conspirators and I were within several weeks of establishing the separate countries of the United Northern States and the United Southern States of America. Why was it so important to you, personally, to stop me from accomplishing this?"

"Because this war is inevitable. You've said many times, Mr. President, that the abomination of slavery must be abolished from the face of the earth."

"But at what price, Mr. Johnson?"

"At any price, Mr. President!"

"So that's the answer, is it? Slavery is an evil that must be destroyed at any price, even if the nation is also destroyed in the process."

"The nation will survive; and you, Mr. President, will lead us through this war with dignity and grace; for who will understand survival better than you?"

Mr. Johnson and his companion knew that it was time to leave. Mrs. Booth left first, with Mr. Johnson, as always, several steps behind. One ... two; One ... two;

"Wait, Mr. Johnson."

The President's aide stopped at the doorway.

"Yes, Mr. President?"

The President arose from his chair and walked over to a small window near the doorway. He put his hands on the ledge, as if to brace himself. For a few moments he peered aimlessly into the courtyard outside. It was getting dark. The empty courtyard was steeped in shadows from a plethora of overhanging vines.

"How does it feel to go home again, Mr. Johnson?"

"I'm not sure that I follow you, Mr. President."

"Perhaps the faintest memory remains. An infant torn from his mother's womb. Cries, recriminations, weeping, screaming. A stranger, in his deepest grief, takes the infant in his arms; a beautiful boy, conceived in violence, through the rape of an angel by an angry vagabond.

"The boy lives, but the mother dies. The stranger has no experience and, perhaps, no aptitude with children. Yet something about this boy; a strange, luminous glowing from deep within, captures the soul of the stranger. He must help this child escape the ignorance and insensibility of the world around him. This boy must have his freedom!

"The stranger is now a man possessed. Having very little money, he arranges to work for the boy's freedom.

For sixty days and nights, with virtually no rest or sleep, he works the ground. He chops wood. He builds but never destroys; and, at last, God enters his soul to tell him that now, for the first time, his life will have meaning.

"When his obligation has been fulfilled he leaves the plantation with the infant in his arms. Destitute and homeless, he trusts in God to lead him to a safe and loving home for the child, who now appears to him to be an extension of the woman he loved with all his heart."

The President turned away from the window to face his aide.

"Mr. Johnson, I expect to see you in my office at nine o'clock tomorrow morning. By then, you will have called on each member of my cabinet to inform him that he is required to attend a meeting in this conference room at ten o'clock, at which time we will draw up the documents of war.

"You will then contact the six generals of the Union army currently in Washington to inform them that their presence is required in this conference room at fourteen hundred hours to discuss the logistics of a protracted war against the South. At sixteen hundred hours I'll meet with the four most competent of these generals to discuss tactics for our immediate thrust into the South. The names of these officers will be given to you during our nine o'clock meeting.

"And now, Mr. Johnson, go home and get some sleep. I promise you that tomorrow will be the longest, most arduous day of your career."

"Mr. President, I …"

"Goodnight, Mr. Johnson. You can say goodnight to your actress friend for me."

"She left the premises, Mr. President. I pray that neither of us will ever see her again."

Mr. Johnson turned to leave, but couldn't resist one final question.

"Mr. President, I don't quite understand. Why would this stranger, I assume that it's you, devote so much time and energy to the child of a slave, no matter who it was? Forgive me, but there are so many illegitimate children running around the plantations, why would you become devoted to this particular child?"

"Perhaps I was moved by his handicap, Mr. Johnson. It was quite severe."

"What handicap? What are you talking about?"

"This child inherited the sins of his father. He was born with a brutally deformed right leg."

Mr. Johnson received this news as if hit with a cannon shot. He staggered to the door to keep from falling. The pieces immediately fell into place. His inherent fascination with the President, the almost laughably easy road to his current role as aide. He had been recommended for the job, but at the time it had seemed strange to him that no one else had even been interviewed. He had assumed that there must have been a multitude of unseen applicants that he had been unaware of.

"Goodnight, Mr. Johnson."

"But Mr. President …"

"Goodnight, Mr. Johnson. We'll never speak of this again."

"I understand, Mr. President. Goodnight, sir."

The war was long and horrible, truly the work of the Devil; yet noble deeds were recorded in every corner of the battlefield, for God was there also; and, in time, the President became a symbol of all that's good and decent in mankind: namely patience, compassion, vision, and persistence.

At the end, he gave his life for his country; or perhaps, as implied in rumblings from certain of his former cabinet members, he was killed in a jealous rage by the husband of a former lover.

In any case, he died in his prime and his memory lives on. The only obvious flaw in his character, it would seem, was his fondness for misfits. Why in heaven's name, for example, would he put so much trust in that dim-witted cripple of an aide? Certainly there were others better qualified. Certainly, he could have done better. But the President's reasons were never revealed. He took them with him to the grave.

Mr. Johnson, it seems, was devastated by the death of his mentor. At the funeral, to the embarrassment of all, he arrived late; then slowly shuffled down the aisle with that pathetic gait of his and literally threw himself upon the casket.

After a few moments he got up and slowly, painfully, dragged his disgusting leg down the aisle and out the door. One ... two; One ... two; One ... two; One ... two; He was never seen or heard from again.

THE END

The Lovers

On the morning of December 1st, 1919, I jumped from the jagged rocks of the cliff into the icy waters that flow beneath my estate. I hope you won't hold it against me; I never intended to hurt anyone. I was impulsive and foolish. I dreamed that you had died on the way to our wedding, and then it happened as I dreamed.

I pulled myself from the river, then staggered through the streets for hours, wondering if I would ever die, until finally I collapsed on the lawn outside my estate. The grass was cold and slimy. It had been snowing throughout the day. The sky was now on fire; so warm and cruel.

As I lay on the cold, wet ground I reached out to you. "My darling, wherever they've taken you, whatever they've done with you, don't leave me here like this. Take my soul with you. Let it comfort you in the place where they've imprisoned you.

"I vowed to never leave you. Am I suddenly to forget my vow? Are the Gods now laughing at us? Were we simply pawns in some perverse, sick game?

"Take me with you, my love; for only in death will I ever again taste the sweetness of life."

I broke down in sobs, knowing that I would never see you again. A neighbor found me shivering in the snow. I was hallucinating. I dreamed that I searched for you in a dilapidated castle.

An elderly caretaker lived in the castle. He seemed to know you. He said you had once lived there, but it was a long time ago. He took me to your room; a candle was still burning.

When I asked where you had gone the caretaker became angry. He said that I asked too many questions, but I could stay in your room if I wanted to. I said that wouldn't be good enough. I begged him to tell me where I could find you. He pointed to the roof.

"He flies through the night."

"But I need to see him. If I can just see him one more time."

"He'll never come back. He's free."

Then I realized you were still in the room. He had lied to me. The candle was still burning.

"Where are you?" I screamed.

The caretaker laughed at me. "He's a flier. He doesn't crawl like you."

"Why are you doing this to me? I don't wish you any harm. Why won't you help me?"

"You're not good enough for him."

"Please don't say that to me. Why are you so cruel?"

"It's my job to be cruel. A soul can't survive unless it's ready to break free and learn to fly. My job is to squeeze the life out of weak and dying souls who refuse to fly. We need the space. There are just too many of them."

He moved closer and began to lick my face with his long, grainy tongue. I threw my hands up to protect myself, but his huge tongue kept fighting its way through my fingers until it penetrated my right nostril, violating it repeatedly with a swift and passionate in-and-out motion. I was terrified that my soul was about to be sucked out through my nose.

"Cecil! Cecil, my darling, what have you found? It's poor Miss Morisot lying in the snow. Oh, Cecil, what's wrong with her? I'm sure she appreciates your kisses, darling, but it's time to get off her now and let mommy have a look. That's a good boy, Cecil. Good boy."

"Oh my, she's sick. I think she has a fever. We have to get her inside and out of these wet clothes. The poor dear. After what she went through with that nice Mr. Johnson getting struck by an automobile and dying right in front of her eyes.

"Oh, Cecil, it's so horrible. Now look at her. She's going to die along with him unless we get her in front of a warm fire. Go get some help, Cecil. Go get Mr. Peck. You know Mr. Peck. He lives on the other side of us. Tell him Miss Morisot is about to die. Oh, Cecil,

I know you can't talk, darling; just bark at him. Make him come with you. Oh, poor Miss Morisot. Hurry, Cecil."

From the moment my soul left my body I began to fly, soaring eagerly up into the bitter cold air above the city. I could see my neighbor's harlequin Great Dane running away from my lifeless body. I tried to keep up with him. My body suddenly reappeared. I put my arms out to my side. I was free.

"Mrs. Ingram, you're going to have to help me. It's too slippery for me to carry her by myself, and I'm certainly not going to drag her all the way to her front door. You'll have to pick her up by her feet and I'll take her by the arms. We've got to get her inside quickly. It may already be too late."

"It's a pity she refuses to keep servants. Just a housekeeper twice a week and, of course, that awful drunkard of a gardener. I know she could afford to ..."

"Mrs. Ingram, take hold of her! We don't have much time."

"But, Mr. Peck ..."

"Just grab her feet."

"Mr. Peck, please ..."

"You can do it, Mrs. Ingram. We can't let her die out here in the snow."

"Mr. Peck, you're so cruel. Do you want me to collapse next to her? Then you'll have to drag both of us."

"Just pick her up and start walking. You don't have to be so dainty, Mrs. Ingram. Just grab her! That's it. Just be careful ... it's slippery."

"I'll never make it. You know I won't. I'll faint dead away. Cecil! Cecil, my darling, help me. Help me, sweet Cecil!"

From the vast, cold distance I could hear the cries of the dreadful beast. Unearthly howling grated my senses. Bony fingers and gnarled knuckles ripped into my armpits. My wings had been clipped; my dream had ended. You were gone forever.

"Don't stop now, Mrs. Ingram. We're almost there."

"Put me down, Mrs. Ingram. Can you imagine what this is doing to your hemorrhoids? We'll have to start carrying you."

"Oh, Cecilia, thank God, you're still alive. Mr. Peck made me do it. He doesn't care about my hemorrhoids."

"Of course he does. Let me ask ... Mr. Peck, do you care about Mrs. Ingram's hemorrhoids?"

"You were dying, my dear; or so we thought."

"I wasn't dying, Mr. Peck; but if you'll put me down I'll let you have your way with me, right here in the snow."

"Cecilia! Are you mad? Mr. Peck is a man of God."

"Mr. Peck is a psychopath. He's been stalking me for weeks. You didn't know that, did you Mrs. Ingram. That's why he moved into the neighborhood. Now, let's see ... Which commandment are you breaking today, Mr. Peck? Thou shalt not lust after thy neighbor?"

"That's not entirely fair, Miss Morisot."

"I bet all this excitement has left Mr. Peck with an erection. Would you have a look, Mrs. Ingram?"

"Cecilia ... really. You're embarrassing me."

"You'll enjoy his performance, Mrs. Ingram; it's quite entertaining. Mr. Peck stands out here every night and moons my bedroom window. After a while he pulls his pants up, gazes up at my window, and begins to sing, 'Let Me Call You Sweetheart.' Then he unzips his pants and masturbates on this poor tree."

"I'll put you down if you wish. Gently, Mrs. Ingram ... gently. That's it. That's it. There you go. I hope you're comfortable lying in the snow. I've always believed in the principles of the Good Samaritan, Miss Morisot. I was simply trying to be a good neighbor. We all know that you suffered a terrible tragedy this morning, but that's no excuse for you to lash out at me like this. Just remember, Miss Morisot ... nothing in this world happens by accident. What happened to Mr. Johnson was God's will."

"That certainly is comforting, Mr. Peck. I feel so much better now."

"I should hope that you do."

"Tell me. Mr. Peck ... Are you going to masturbate anytime soon? Mrs. Ingram and I would like to watch."

"Don't do this, please ..,."

"Don't do what, Mr. Peck?"

"Please, Miss Morisot. I'm begging ..."

"Then take me up on my offer; that is … if you're man enough. Are you man enough, Mr. Peck? It'll be our little snow fuck. If you're nice, I might even let you stick it up my …"

"Cecilia! I'm appalled!"

I could feel my strength returning. On a whim I hopped onto the palms of my hands, then slowly and sensually wrapped my legs around my neck. I realize I was foolish to reveal my powers, but what difference did it make anymore? You were gone, my darling. My life was over, though I was doomed to live.

I began to walk briskly on my hands up the icy pathway to my estate. The harlequin beast, now barking furiously, attempted to lunge for my face. I turned my eyes sharply toward the animal and addressed him by his real name.

"Would you like to chew on my face, Rufonzo? Is that it? You're mine now, Rufonzo. Do you really think it's wise to piss me off? What's this … foaming at the mouth? You've got to be kidding. Why don't you just back off and enjoy your last few moments on earth? Go lie down somewhere; I'll come for you when I'm ready.

"Ouch! You annoying bastard! You know … this may surprise you, but I haven't been myself lately. I was going to be nice; but if you snap at my face one more time I'll impale you by your knees. I'll roast you on a spit."

"Stay back, Mrs. Ingram; it's worse than I could have imagined. Oh, God, it's beautiful. To see her in her true form. Oh, Jesus … just a minute. Forgive me. Oh … Oh … Oh! Shit!

"Ahhhhhhhhh!"

"Mr. Peck? Mr. Peck, what did you just do? Mr. Peck? Mr. Peck? Mr. Peck, answer me. What did you just do? Mr. Peck …?"

"I ejaculated all over this tree. What do you think I just did?"

"But, Mr. Peck … how terribly inappropriate."

"I'm in love with her. I can't help it."

"But … What's wrong with you? She's just our neighbor, Mr. Peck. You make her seem like a…"

"Just our neighbor, Mrs. Ingram? Just our neighbor? Hold on … Oh shit."

"Again, Mr. Peck?"

"Oh, shit …"

"There you go again … whacking away. Honestly, Mr. Peck, this is beyond all sense of decency and propriety. You should be ashamed of …"

"I'm yours, baby …"

"Mr. Peck? Are you addressing me?"

"Ride it, baby. Ride it!"

"Mr. Peck, you're hysterical. Look at you! You're crying."

"Yes … Yes, Jesus!"

"I must say, Mr. Peck … I've never witnessed such an exhibition."

"Ah … Ah … Ah … Ah …"

"Let it fly, Mr. Peck."

"Ahhhhhhhhh! God! Jesus! Damn …"

"Mr. Peck, you have lust in your heart!"

"I'm caught in her web. Why don't you just leave me the hell alone."

"Are you a cycle path, Mr. Peck?"

"He who has ears, let him hear."

"I have ears, Mr. Peck. Rather dainty ones, I might add."

"Do you have eyes, Mrs. Ingram? Can't you see? We're in the presence of evil!"

"What evil can you possibly …"

"Oh dear Lord, Mrs. Ingram, open your eyes! Trapped between life and death … an aberration so cruel that even Satan himself has forsaken her. Miss Morisot is the Undead."

"The Unwhat? Come, Cecil. We must run from this terrible woman."

"Stand your ground, Mrs. Ingram. We have nothing to fear if we trust in the Almighty God."

"But, how can she be the Undead? I've seen her cavorting around in the daylight. I've spoken to her at social gatherings."

"She's not a vampire, Mrs. Ingram. The Undead drinks tea, not blood."

"Now I remember; she must be a witch. I've seen her holding her broomstick."

"While sweeping her porch, perhaps. No, Mrs. Ingram, it's not as you think. The Undead, when provoked, can crawl like a lizard at great speed; but the Undead has no capacity to fly."

"Ahhhh … My Cecil! She's burning him! Oh, Cecil … bury yourself in the snow."

"He's no longer your Cecil, Mrs Ingram. He's an emissary from Hell … a beast. His true name is Rufonzo. I know him. He was a scholar in the Ancient Order of the Brotherhood; that is, until he raped his sister and murdered her lover. His fate is sealed. I know the power of the Undead, Mrs. Ingram. I've held the sacred scrolls in my hands."

… and the gates of Hell shall open wide and jam tight against the pillars of death.

Satan's beasts, mad with fear and desire, shall rush the gates and attempt to claw their way to earth. Only a few shall survive the slaughter of the gates to ravage the earth once more.

But woe unto those who escape from Hell, for the lair of the Undead is all of earth; and their hideous cries shall be silenced forever by the Godless hand of Satan's own daughter.

"Oh, Cecil, you must tell her you're from Heaven. Eat the snow, my love. It will cool you off."

"The Undead sleeps with the angels, Mrs. Ingram. The Undead sucks the souls of the innocent. By assimilating the soul of the God-fearing Mr. Johnson she must have satisfied her lust for love; but I can assure you that true love is impossible for the Undead."

"Cecil, darling ... your balls are on fire!"

"Mrs. Ingram, must you resort to gutter language?"

"Balls afire!"

"Avert your eyes, Mrs. Ingram."

"Oh, Cecil, you must stop your barking. Even the castrati have a deeper timbre than you."

"Yip, yip ... woof ..."

"You can look now, Mrs. Ingram. The immolation is complete. The beast has been annihilated."

"The beast has risen, Mr. Peck. You certainly did your best to keep me alive; but, then, what would your life be like without me? No fantasy, no excitement, no sex? Tell me, Mr. Peck, is it God's will that I walk the earth? No, don't answer. I may be tempted to remove your tongue. I'm sorry about your animal, Mrs. Ingram; I had no choice. Now leave me."

I walked upright to my front door, then crawled through the parlor and up the stairs to my bedroom. You came to me in a vision as I lay shivering on the floor. You knelt in front of me and called my name. I looked up into your eyes ... so haunted, so beautiful.

A single tear rolled down your cheek. You leaned over and whispered something in my ear, but in a strange language ... the language of the dead. I begged you not to leave. You smiled and put your finger to your lips. Then you walked to the open window and flew into the night. It was the last time I would ever see you.

I woke up several hours later in a horrible sweat. My fever had intensified in the night; my muscles ached, my tongue had blistered; but I had to be ready. They would come for me now.

I never told you the truth about me, my darling, and yet after all these years I want you to know. I was born in the fires of the great plagues of the 14th century. My father was Cardinal Rottaglia, the most powerful man in Italy. My mother was a street wench, a common whore.

As an infant I was left for dead on the streets of Rome. As I lay there, half eaten by rats, a man approached me and picked me up by my hair. I learned later that no one in his right mind would have dared to walk into the fires of the plague. To touch my unclean body would have meant certain death to any man.

But this was not any man. It was Florio, the Angel of Agony. Florio bathed my wounds with erotic oil, which he had stolen from Euphoria, the Angel of Ecstacy. Erotic oil was so powerful that it could cure the plague within seconds; but if you applied too much it would cause insanity.

The Angel of Ecstacy had a notoriously bad temper along with an excess of supernatural powers. To avoid her wrath, I was taken immediately to a bordello in the south of France where I was raised in the techniques of whores. I was studious and attentive, and by the age of fifteen had graduated to the most prestigious brothel in Paris.

Euphoria was so impressed with my showmanship and advanced technical abilities that she decided to entrust me with a small portion of her responsibilities. She appointed me "Whore to the Angels," and for the next five years I was forbidden to have sexual contact with other humans.

After polishing my skills on the lesser angels I was ready for a more formidable task. I was assigned to sleep with the highest officials of the Church of Rome. For the first time in my life I was deeply afraid, for the extraordinary cruelty of the Cardinals was well known to those in my profession. In desperation, I ran to Euphoria's boudoir and begged her to reconsider and let me live out my youth as "Whore to the Angels." Euphoria laughed in my face.

"You should be grateful, my sweet; it shows that I have confidence in you. Anyway, it's time for you to move on. The angels are such a boring lay."

"But only an angel can tame the fury of the priests."

"Then I'll give you an advantage."

"An advantage?"

"The power of rejuvenation. Eternal life. Whatever you'd like to call it. Just don't bore me with technicalities."

Before I could say a word, Euphoria flicked out her tongue and wedged it between my lips. A bolt of energy slammed into my body with such violence that I levitated several feet in the air and began giggling and doing cartwheels on the player piano. Though I had never known the taste of liquor, I jumped up onto the bar and began spouting bawdy drinking songs while slapping my ass.

"Come and get it, you bastards! ***Oh, roll me over in the clover …***"

After two or three minutes my body became rigid and I experienced intense, multiple orgasms. Finally, I dropped to the floor and fell fast asleep. When I awoke, Euphoria was lying naked next to me.

"You're such a bore. Twenty years old and you've never had an orgasm until now. You've never even been kissed."

"But how did you …"

"Something I'm famous for. I zapped you with erotic oil hidden on the tip of my tongue."

"You almost killed me."

"I had to stop your whining. It's most unbecoming for an angel."

"You have the power to glorify?"

"It's not exactly glorious, my lovely. The males, especially, are such a weak, effeminate lot. They'll urinate on you while you sleep, for you were once their whore. They adore the spectacle of crucifixion; but, in your case, they've chosen gang rape."

"They wouldn't dare."

"They'll come for you tonight. The flutter of their wings will sound like an army of locusts. Close your ears and your eyes, my pretty; let them have their fun. They'll try to tear you apart, but they can't destroy you.

I've glorified you specifically to provide sexual pleasure to the masses. Even the angels can't hurt you now."

"Then I'm really one of them?"

"I wouldn't gloat just yet. I've assigned you to an eternity of orgasmic pleasure, but I may just as well have sent you straight into Hell. You'll never know what it's like to love and be loved by just one person; your assignment is to love them all. And, of course, you'll never have wings. That has to come from a higher source. Anyway, once the angels see that you're still a whore they'll probably stop bothering you."

"But ... to never fall in love?"

"Don't test my patience, little one. Love was never meant for you. Love is for the weepers, the intellectuals, the poets. If you fall in love I'll have lost you, and I'll never stand for that. Besides ... your lover will grow old without you; not a pretty sight."

"Then what do you expect of me?"

"I expect you to do what whores do. What kind of a question is that? I've given you eternal youth, and I expect you to be goddamn grateful. Why else would an angel lie next to a whore? Hell, I might get the plague."

"What are you ...? Why are you doing this?"

"Don't play the innocent with me, you little slut. You're still a whore. And guess what? Your angelic little butt will be humping humans for all eternity; I've seen to that. Now get out the tongue. I want it sloppy and with great passion. Bow down and worship your God, my pretty one."

At that moment, the Angel of Agony flew into the room (quite literally) and attacked Euphoria with a huge container of erotic oil, which quickly soaked into her scalp and ran into her eyes. Euphoria at first appeared confused and began to scoot around on her back while panting like a dog.

Suddenly, she rose to her knees and began to vigorously shake her breasts from side to side, then up and down, and finally in a broad circular motion. She began shouting, to no one in particular, "Am I beautiful? Am I beautiful? Do you mean it or are you just saying it? Damn, I'm horny."

When no one answered, she stopped jiggling and began to quietly survey the room, as if determined to pounce on anything that even remotely protruded from the wall or the floor or, for that matter, the ceiling. Finally, in desperation, she wobbled to her feet, placed her hands on her hips, and for the next several hours hopped up and down on one leg while kicking the other leg high in the air.

This ritual was well known in those days as one of the best possible ways to release sexual tension. It never caught on with men, but women of all ages practiced it faithfully as a primitive form of birth control (as it would invariably lead to a migraine later in the evening). Years later it was reintroduced into Parisian society as a form of dance called the "Can-Can."

I jumped up onto Florio's back, and the two of us rose quickly as the Angel of Agony spread his ample wings. Florio was not allowed into Heaven however. We flew into the depths of Hell, where Florio had always wanted to go anyway. It wasn't that Florio was evil. It's just that he had always believed he could bring comfort to those who needed it most: the denizens of Hell.

But when Florio arrived in Hell he discovered the true meaning of agony. His wings caught on fire and burned down to a single feather on each side. For the rest of eternity he would flap each feather as hard as he could in a futile attempt to fly out of Hell; but, as so many of us have learned, Hell is a labyrinth from which there is no escape.

I was surprised to find that the most powerful members of the Ancient Order of the Brotherhood had recently taken up residence in Hell. The Brotherhood's sole reason for existing was to learn everything there is to know. Unfortunately, they already knew everything, so they were really getting bored. The only thing that kept them going (outside of gastric stimulation) was the knowledge that they would soon merge with God; and, if everything went according to their calculations, at the exact moment they merged with God they would actually become God.

Their plan was severely disrupted, though, when a few of the elders decided to meet for dinner one night at a Mexican restaurant near Tijuana. Apparently, one of them got into the Mescal and made a pitch to convince the others that they should all just become God right then and there. Another one poured so much salsa on his frijoles that he needed to stand up and walk around for a while out in the desert.

Before they realized it the whole group found themselves out in the desert, sitting around a campfire, singing Kumbaya. From there it seemed a logical step to actually begin the process of becoming God (I assume by funneling into protoplasm, or perhaps by breathing large amounts of ether). Unfortunately, they woke up in Hell instead.

With its leaders gone, the Brotherhood fell into the hands of the fundamentalists, and quickly became a bastion of bombastic and pompous self-righteousness. In time it became the voice of Elias P. Peck, the most obnoxious pulpit pounder who ever lived. Elias P. Peck devoted his ministry to the condemnation of sex. He preached that sex was to be used only sparingly as a means of procreation; and, even then, should be practiced in absolute darkness with no hint of pleasure.

Eventually, he was banned by the Brotherhood because of his penchant for inappropriate language. Words like sex slave, whoremonger, and smut peddler punctuated all his conversations. It became especially difficult to accommodate him at the Brotherhood's annual awards dinners, as he would constantly jump up from his table and yell, "Harlot!" or "Sodomist!" at the wives of the honored guests.

Shortly before he was expelled, Mr. Peck studied the Brotherhood's records and discovered that a seemingly innocent young woman, then living in an upscale neighborhood in Vermont, was actually the infamous "Whore to the Angels." He became incensed and took it upon himself to expose my identity to the world.

The next morning he created a large placard which simply stated "Whore," followed by an exclamation point. He then traveled to my estate by rail, holding his placard up in the air to keep it from getting damaged. (I understand that he was slapped several times by female passengers.)

When he arrived in Vermont, he positioned himself with his placard on the sidewalk in front of my estate, determined to reveal my true identity to anyone who happened to walk by. Later that afternoon, as I returned from a visit to the local humane society, Mr. Peck stepped out from behind a shrub and began to castigate me for the sin of fornication. He was in his glory all right, but he had made one fatal mistake: he had allowed himself to confront me without witnesses.

I recalled a conversation with Euphoria, hundreds of years previously, in which she had revealed the secret to "Sexitis," an extremely potent spell that she had invented to use only on the most irritating and sanctimonious priests. Sexitis is the unquenchable need to humiliate yourself in the most outrageous manner. I decided to experiment with my magical powers and turn Elias P. Peck into a harmless sexual buffoon. I asked him if he would be willing to hop all the way home like a frog. His reply was predictable.

"Get thee behind me, Satan!"

"I'd like you to undress, Mr. Peck. Then take your underwear and hold it up like a flag."

"I shall not enter into the work of the Devil!"

"Oh yes you shall, Mr. Peck. Oh yes, you shall. Do it now, Mr. Peck. You heard me. That's right. Completely naked, Mr. Peck. That's it. Now start hopping. On your mark, get set, go!"

Mr. Peck hopped off into the distance at a most impressive speed. When he arrived at the end of the block, he stood up and waved his underwear at passersby. I didn't see Mr. Peck again for several days, but I heard talk around town of a strange "hopping man."

It proved to be quite disconcerting to the town's elite as, apparently, Mr. Peck loved to hide in the shrubs and hop out at people as they walked by. The local police tried for days to corral him, but he proved impossible to catch as he had developed the ability to hop at incredible speeds (partly, I'm sure, out of the need to protect himself from adverse publicity).

After a few days I took pity on Mr. Peck and summoned him to my home. He arrived naked and hopping mad.

"Have you enjoyed your stay in Vermont, Mr. Peck?"

"I can't say that I have."

"Do you think, perhaps, it's time for you to leave?"

"I intend to stay."

"For what reason, Mr. Peck?"

"To protect the world from the evil within these walls."

"Go home, Mr. Peck. You're out of your depth. Go back where you belong. If you refuse, I promise you that your situation will become infinitely worse."

"How could it possibly get worse?"

"Don't tempt me, Mr. Peck."

"Oh, wretched princess! Defiler of angels! The seed of Satan rises from your loins!"

Why did he have to tempt me? "Inside your rectum, Mr. Peck, there's an incredible itch. It seems to flare up during your sidewalk sermons. From now on, Mr. Peck, your sanctimonious outbursts will be accompanied by an overwhelming need to scratch. I surmise that at least five or six fingers will be needed to put out the fire."

"Fornicator! Daughter of Satan! Repent! Repent! Repent ....

"Ahh! Ahh! Ahh! Ooooohh! Ooooohh! Ooooohh! Ooooohh!"

"Wow ... both hands."

"Ooooohh! Ooooohh! Ahhhhhh!"

"I guess you needed that sixth finger after all."

"Ahhhhhh! Ooooohh!"

"Go home, Mr. Peck. I'll release you from the spell, but if I ever see you again ..."

I released Elias P. Peck. He received his clothes and walked out into the world; but he would never be free to torment me again. I had forgotten: Sexitis is irreversible.

Over the next few weeks Mr. Peck performed his outrageous sexual humiliation for my entertainment, though I tried several times to persuade him to leave town and return to familiar surroundings. But Sexitis had produced a strange and baffling by-product: Mr. Peck had fallen hopelessly in love with me. His eyes would glaze over in adulation every time he looked at me. His obsession was absolute.

I watched this transition in amazement, for I was completely ignorant of love. I had never felt the slightest twinge of love for anyone. Was love an obsession? Was love the need to ravish another person? Was it the need to be ravished by your beloved? It was something I could never know. But then why did you ask me to love you, my darling? Why did you make such an impossible request?

In the short time we were together I learned so many things: I learned that love is the call from another world, another lifetime. Love carries you into a world that never existed, that never will exist; and yet to that world you vow your very existence.

What happens to two people in love, my darling? What makes them so different from everyone else? From the moment their eyes first meet they'll live in a world that no man or woman can ever touch. Only their spirits will be allowed to enter and intertwine and ravish and rest; and only in that world will they learn the truth about themselves: that their spirits are their true selves, and the world that never existed is the only world there is.

Love transcends death, my darling. Through all these years I've never stopped wanting you, needing you; that's the spell you cast on me. Love is even stronger than Sexitis. That's why Mr. Peck should have learned to resist my commands. The stronger urge cancels out the weaker.

They came for me the next day, the morning after I lost you; I knew they would. A crowd gathered in the square outside of City Hall. After a while they started walking in the direction of my estate; I could see them from my balcony. A few were wielding clubs. Mr. Peck was standing next to his favorite tree in my front yard.

"They're coming for you, my dear … hundreds of them. Mrs. Ingram told the whole town. There's no escape for you now. I strongly suggest that you make your peace with the Almighty. Your evil career is about to end forever."

"Haven't you noticed something, Mr. Peck?"

"Noticed what?"

"They're almost here and you still have your clothes on."

"No! For God's sake, no!"

"Hurry, Mr. Peck."

"Please don't …"

"Completely naked, Mr. Peck. Hurry! That's it. How's your singing voice today?"

"For God's sake …"

"Hands on hips. Bend backward."

"No! Please!

"Sing it, Mr. Peck."

"Please, Miss Morisot ..."

"Now!"

"Let me call you sweetheart ..."

"Work it, Mr. Peck!"

"Ah ... Ah ... Ah ... Ah ... Ahhhhhhhhh! God! Shit! Jesus ..."

Mr. Peck was hauled off in handcuffs. I crawled down the staircase and out the back door. There was no time to pack.

A few of them chased me through the woods, but I could crawl a lot faster than they could run. One of them tried to outsmart me by anticipating which direction I would take. I crawled up a tree and watched him distance himself from the pack.

What in the world was he trying to prove? He had a knife and a club. I had the ability to crush the life out of him simply by dropping out of the tree and wrapping my legs around his neck.

I'm not immune to stabbings and beatings. I'd need some time to heal, but I'd remember; and if he got away I'd come for him. But this one was luckier than most. He never found me.

And so I move from town to town, from country to country; never aging, never changing, never staying long enough for anyone to notice. An apartment in San Francisco, a hotel room in Barcelona. A villa in St. Tropez.

I have lots of dates, but just for sex; always for sex. But not because I want to. Because I have to. It's what I am.

"Some night soon, my darling, when the stars are out and you hear me crying, come and visit me as you did once before, all those years ago. Look into my eyes once again and call my name. Just remember, my darling, I'm here waiting for you. I'll always wait for you. It's who I am."

THE END